Poetry Explorers

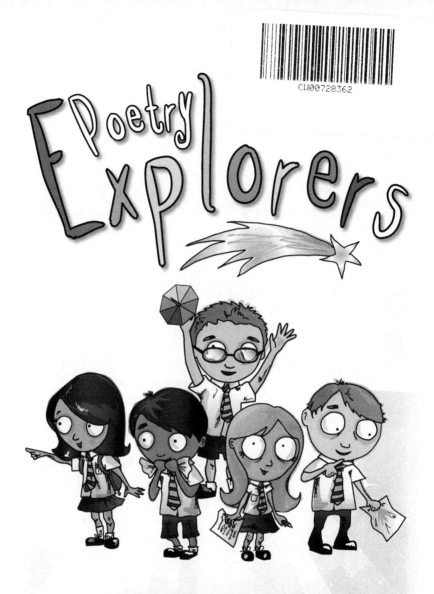

North & East Scotland

Edited by Claire Tupholme

First published in Great Britain in 2009 by

 Young**Writers**

Remus House
Coltsfoot Drive
Peterborough
PE2 9JX
Telephone: 01733 890066
Website: www.youngwriters.co.uk

Foreword

At Young Writers our defining aim is to promote an enjoyment of reading and writing amongst children and young adults. By giving aspiring poets the opportunity to see their work in print, their love of the written word as well as confidence in their own abilities has the chance to blossom.

Our latest competition Poetry Explorers was designed to introduce primary school children to the wonders of creative expression. They were given free reign to write on any theme and in any style, thus encouraging them to use and explore a variety of different poetic forms.

We are proud to present the resulting collection of regional anthologies which are an excellent showcase of young writing talent. With such a diverse range of entries received, the selection process was difficult yet very rewarding. From comical rhymes to poignant verses, there is plenty to entertain and inspire within these pages. We hope you agree that this collection bursting with imagination is one to treasure.

Contents

Scotstoun School, Bridge of Don

Strachan Primary School, Banchory

Strathdon School, Strathdon

The Poems

A Parrot

There once lived a parrot named Kipper
Who was on a diet of chicken dippers
He got fatter and fatter
And thought it didn't matter
But he didn't fit into his pink fluffy slippers.

Holly Walton–Jones (8)
Carlogie Primary School, Carnoustie

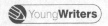

Pirate

P irate overboard
I sland in sight
R um swirling in the barrel
A mazing cannonballs blasting
T reasure sparkling in the night
E xcited pirates partying.

Abby Selfridge (8)
Carlogie Primary School, Carnoustie

Pirates

P arrots fly in the sky
I am called Jim
R um is great
A nd pirates fight
T reasure is so shiny
E ye patches are black
S hips are huge.

Amy Harris (8)
Carlogie Primary School, Carnoustie

Dim Tim

There once was a pirate called Tim,
Who battled and lost a limb.
He didn't like rum,
But loved playing the drum
And was also enormously dim.

Theo Kyriacou (8)
Carlogie Primary School, Carnoustie

Treasure Chest

T he pirates think they are cod,
R oger is my friend,
E ye patch on my eye,
A mazing treasure,
S hooting cannons,
U sed an axe,
R ocks are jagged,
E xcellent gold.

Aillie Townsend (9)
Carlogie Primary School, Carnoustie

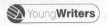

Jim White

There once was a pirate, Jim White
Who had a great big fright.
He got punched in the face
And couldn't tie his shoelace,
But he still was able to write.

Sam Strachan (8)

Carlogie Primary School, Carnoustie

Pirates

P arrot eating his hair.
I sland in sight captain.
R um was his favourite thing.
A nd also hated his crew.
T reasure hidden in the ground.
E xciting finding the captain's treasure.

Chloe Brown (9)

Carlogie Primary School, Carnoustie

The Pirate From Beijing

There once was a pirate from Beijing,
Who did a very cool thing.
He found a crown,
He did the opposite of frown,
Now he is the king.

Michael Jamieson (9)
Carlogie Primary School, Carnoustie

Pirate

P arrots squawking
I sland of fun
R ocks on the sand
A pples on the tree
T reasure map
E scape in his pirate ship.

Daragh Connor (10)

Carlogie Primary School, Carnoustie

Jim And The Bin

There once was a pirate called Jim
He liked to take out the bin
He tipped it over the side
And had a very big slide
And landed on a shark's fin.

Rebecca Bell (9)

Carlogie Primary School, Carnoustie

A Pirate Called Jack

There once was a pirate called Jack
Who had a really big sack
With lots of treasure
Which was a pleasure
Which he wouldn't give back.

Jack O'Connor (8)
Carlogie Primary School, Carnoustie

Dog Kennings

Paper-chewer
Garden runner
Fence-jumper
Postman-barker
Sofa-chomper
Bowl-breaker
Cat-chaser.

Iain Baxter (10)

Charleston Primary School, Aberdeen

The Jungle

In the jungle where the hollow trees sit
Black apes swing on long green vines
While huge cats run, crouch, pounce and eat
Small poison scorpions wander in the tall grass
And rhinos rub their horns on the towering trees.

Strange and scary noises echo through
The amazing beautiful green wilderness
Elephant's feet bang and pound through the jungle
So much to see, hear and find.

Robbie Borthwick (11)
Charleston Primary School, Aberdeen

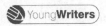

Tartan

T artan is bright
A lways through the night
R ed, blue and yellow too
T oo many patterns to see
A tartan for every name
N ever forget tartan's the best.

Sally Cheyne (11)
Charleston Primary School, Aberdeen

Concert — Haiku

Bright shining lights flash
Banging, rocking guitarists
Fans scream, people jump.

Cassie Cowper (10)
Charleston Primary School, Aberdeen

Cat

Leg-brusher
Mouse-trapper
Flea-catcher
Milk-drinker
Night-stalker
Purr-maker
Fur-licker
Food-stealer.

Craig Johnson (11)
Charleston Primary School, Aberdeen

The Jungle

There was an orange, slimy snake
With a roaring lion cub.
The long rustling grass under my feet
And the sky above.

The monkeys were swinging from the branches,
The hippo was prancing along in the mud bath.
The tall trees swaying in the wind
And now the jungle is sleeping, no sound.

Nicola Lyon (10)
Charleston Primary School, Aberdeen

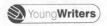

Panda

Eyes-punched
Feet-stomped
Human-cuddler
Bamboo-eater
Asia-roamer
Ear-picker.

Liam Malcolm (10)
Charleston Primary School, Aberdeen

Football

I'm running with my football
Heading to the goal I go
I am running as fast as I can
Trying to keep the flow.

Further and further I go
Past the halfway line
Now I'm in the box,
It's my time to shine.

I'm pulling back my foot
Away to hit the ball
I look up at the keeper
He is very tall.

I'm feeling very anxious
To see if I have scored
I see the ball hit the net
'Goal!' the crowd roared.

Aaron McDonald (10)
Charleston Primary School, Aberdeen

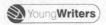
The Loch Ness Monster

Up in the Highlands lives the Loch Ness Monster,
Getting crowded by the paparazzi taking pictures.
His long, scaly, hairy body resting across the water,
He fishes along the murky, cold water looking for food.

He sleeps at the bottom of the sea peacefully,
But gets angry with all the noise up at the shore.
People have tried to find him but have not succeeded.
Do you think he is mythical?

Ruby Menzies (10)
Charleston Primary School, Aberdeen

Cheerleading

C heering is what the audience do
H appiness when we win
E xcitement when there's a competition
E ncouragement is what we get
R hythm is what we need for dance
L earning new moves is really fun
E mbarrassment when you do it wrong
A wards when we win
D etermination we all have
I nto the arena we all go
N ew talents we will show
G etting our trophies when we win.

Megan Mitchell (10)
Charleston Primary School, Aberdeen

Cat And Dog

Dog,
Fluffy, smooth,
Running, walking, eating,
Beggar, canine, prowler, purrer,
Purring, scratching, cleaning,
Smooth, furry,
Cat.

April Povey (11)

Charleston Primary School, Aberdeen

Siberian Husky

Mane-scratcher
Snow-player
Food-beggar
Sledge-puller
Tail-chaser
Paw-scratcher
Lead-puller
Hole-digger

What am I? - Siberian Husky.

Rebecca Rezin (12)

Charleston Primary School, Aberdeen

Cat And Dog

Cat,
Furry, cuddly,
Purring, playing, scratching,
Crazy, loving, eating, panting,
Speeding, slumping, racing,
Funny, exciting,
Dog.

Olivia Robbie (10)

Charleston Primary School, Aberdeen

Super Car Racing

S peeding in the saleen
U p the hill I go
P assing the other cars
E njoying the big race
R acing round the bends.

C aterham just spun off
A scari V12 just hit the ditch
R oaring on the straights.

R evving my engine
A udi R8 went into the pit
C orvette's engine roaring
I n my face, tyre spin
N early crashing into a ditch
G oing past the finish line.

Andrew Ross (11)
Charleston Primary School, Aberdeen

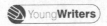

Usian Bolt

U sian Bolt is the fastest man in the world
S uper speed he used in the race
I n his Nike shoes
A mazing speed, he is as fast as lightning
N ow he is famous worldwide.

B eijing 2008 he won gold medals
O n top of the podium
L osers on the bottom
T he best ever runner in the world is Usian Bolt.

Cameron Smith (10)
Charleston Primary School, Aberdeen

The Jungle

The crazy world of the jungle
With animals galore,
Monkeys playing and lions roaring
Snakes slithering, *hiss*.

At night it's quiet but the day is noisy
Trees and exotic plants grow,
The crazy jungle is off to bed
But the only animal awake is the outstanding owl.

Hannah Spink (10)
Charleston Primary School, Aberdeen

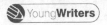

King Cobra

Fear-machine
Rat-trap
Sticking-serpent
Death-master
Heart-stopper
Amazing-tracker.

Dean Sutherland (10)

Charleston Primary School, Aberdeen

Ice And Fire

Ice,
Slippery, cold,
Freezing, shivering, slipping,
Breeze, wind, sparks, flames,
Boiling, roaring, burning,
Warm, hot,
Fire.

Ellie Turnbull (11)
Charleston Primary School, Aberdeen

Tennis

T ennis balls that they use,
E ach day and night they play.
N ext time at Wimbledon Andy Murray will play.
N oon is when they get tired.
I think I am going to sleep.
S oon I am going to be playing.

Arran Watson (11)

Charleston Primary School, Aberdeen

Aberdeen

Aberdeen, Aberdeen, Scotland's third largest city,
With lochs, parks and beaches so pretty,
The River Dee, The River Don,
The both of them are so long,
The anglers in the river,
Catching the catch of the day,
Whilst the bathers catch the sun's rays,
At the harbour the boats come past,
When they toot their horns it's packed with a blast.

Stuart Watson (11)

Charleston Primary School, Aberdeen

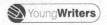

Space

Dark
Scary, peaceful
Black, cold, moonlight
In the sky, is very beautiful
Spinning, exploring, noisy
Running, hungry
Earth.

Cameron Edmonston (9)

Culross Primary School, Culross

Mermaid

M ermaids dance in the beautiful blue sea
E xploring the magic Earth beneath us
R esting on the ragged rocks
M agic creatures following her
A lways peaceful, always smiling
I sland hopping, graceful swimming
D olphin gazing under the sparkling sun.

Katie McKinley (9)
Culross Primary School, Culross

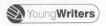

Jungle

J ungle is a dangerous place
U nderground there are worms
N ever go too near a lion
G o near a tiger and you'll be its tea
L eopards are very scary
E ven the little babies!

Sarah Byers (9)

Culross Primary School, Culross

Hobbies

H obbies are good to do,
O nc hobby or two,
B est toys,
B est games,
I like hobbies,
E xcited what to do,
S uper fun.

Kelda McKenzie (8)
Culross Primary School, Culross

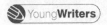

Time Travel

Where will I go, future or past?
I really don't know.
Shall I ask?
I think I might go
To the future,
No, to the past.
I think I'll
Go to the future,
I've made up my mind -
At last.

Lily Pearson (8)
Culross Primary School, Culross

Time Travel

Where should I go?
Just where should I go?
To the future or the past?
Well I don't know!
Maybe I should go to both,
Or maybe none at all.
But I do not know where to go.
The future or the past?
Well I don't know.

Ross La Trobe (8)
Culross Primary School, Culross

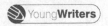

My Hamster

My hamster is cute,
My hamster is sweet.
My hamster loves to eat fruit,
My hamster is the best animal to meet.
My hamster is soft and kind,
If you hurt it, it will not mind.
My hamster is called Ruby,
Sometimes it can get a bit moody!
I love my hamster!

Holly Smith (8)
Culross Primary School, Culross

My Pal

Slipper stealer
Rat killer
Spoon licker
Fast runner
Fun friend
Best pal
Stone picker
Ball buster
Tail wagger
Hay jumper.

Cameron Wilson (8)
Culross Primary School, Culross

My Sister

Super-shopper
DS-pincher
Make-up-wearer
Most-annoying
Music-lover
Nail-painter
Nose-picker
Copy-cat.

Bryony Harris (9)
Culross Primary School, Culross

My Dog Brucie

B rucie is my dog
R unning in the field
U nder the table he goes
C hicken is his favourite
I love him so much
E ven when he barks.

Campbell Bowen (8)
Culross Primary School, Culross

My Cat

Tree-climber
Mouse-catcher
Super-hider
High-jumper
Fast-eater
Toy-lover.

Erin Williams (8)

Culross Primary School, Culross

Love

Sweet and kind
Always on my mind

We could be,
We should be,
Together,
Forever!

Just you and me!

Georgia Watts (9)
Culross Primary School, Culross

Space

Darkness
Meteor showers
Asteroids floating past
Meteor crashed! Destroyed engine!
Signal for help
Waiting hours
Found.

Liam Wright (9)
Culross Primary School, Culross

My Dog

Cat hater
Toy chaser
Footprint leaver
Big barker
Food eater
Face licker
Tail wagger
Super stealer
Bone biter
A good friend.

John Dodds (8)

Culross Primary School, Culross

Hobbies

H obbies are fun things,
O h yes, they're brilliant things.
B asketball is boring,
B owling is okay.
I like football as a hobby,
E xciting, some hobbies,
S wimming is fun as well.

Ryan Mack (8)

Culross Primary School, Culross

My Dog

Washing machine-hater
Grass-muncher
Milk-licker
Rabbit-hunter
Chicken-lover
Jumping-frenzy
Bottle-chewer.

Aaron Waite

Culross Primary School, Culross

The Sardinian Sun

The waves crash against the rocks,
It seems someone is drawing them back in again.
A sudden urge pushes them back towards the beach,
The sun shines down making the sea sparkle.
Listen, you can hear the call of the sea, just like a shantie.

Georgia Harris (11)
Culross Primary School, Culross

The Jungle

J ungle full of wonderful and mysterious animals.
U rania butterflies fly silently by.
N atives live in the deep dark part of the forest,
G orillas, big, hairy and strong animals,
L eaping leopards are fast and furious.
E merald tree boas blend in with the grass. Scary!

Aaron McKinley (11)
Culross Primary School, Culross

Big Foot

B iggest creature in all the land
I maginative creature
G iant foot size of a car

F urriest creature to roam the Earth
O n he goes back to his cave
O ut in the forests
T wenty foot tall.

Declan Hood (10)

Culross Primary School, Culross

The Dragon!

The dragon is ferocious!
The dragon is green!
The dragon is red-eyed!
The dragon is mean!

The dragon's teeth are like kitchen knives!
The dragon's teeth are like razor-sharp blades!
The dragon's roar is like a thunderstorm.

The dragon's body is large and beastly,
The dragon's body is strong and mighty,
The dragon is fearless and brave.

Lewis Aird (11)
Culross Primary School, Culross

My Cat

Big sleeper
Very energetic
Big eater
Very furry
Tree climber
Mad player
Cool cat
Big ears
Black coloured
Mouse chaser.

Ruairidh Gordon (11)

Culross Primary School, Culross

Weather

Wind blows and rain drops
Sun shines and snow falls
The weather is rough
The weather is tough
The weather, there are so many kinds.

Lightning strikes
Thunder rumbles
Hailstones clatter
Black clouds splatter
In the sky is where we see it
The weather, the weather, that's me.

Alexander Boggon (10)
Culross Primary School, Culross

The Sea

Dolphins dancing in the sun,
Whales singing their songs under the star,
Magical and beautiful the soul of the sea,
Endlessly the waves crash against the shore, the tide never sleeps.

Carly Bowen (11)
Culross Primary School, Culross

My Brother

Hair heavy!
Big bully!
Super spotty!
Tall teen!
Vicious vampire!
Geeky gamer!

Erin Malcolm (10)
Culross Primary School, Culross

The Black Dragon

Today I saw a dragon
With teeth as sharp as needles,
He was the height of the Eiffel Tower
With black glowing eyes.

His wings were strong
He was coloured black,
His tail was so rough it made a wave sound
When he moved.

The dragon moved as quick as lightning
With his bumpy scales rattling as he moved,
The head had ears which were quite big,
He had gigantic muscles,
He also looked quite scary.

He turned around to look at me and said,
'Dearie, would you like a cup of tea?'

Caitlin Collins (9)
Kinghorn Primary School, Kinghorn

The Dragon Poem

Today I saw a dragon, it had golden teeth,
Its scaly wings moved swiftly like clouds moving in the sky.
He had immense eyes,
Each one the size of three red bloodshot bowling balls.
The dragon was dark pink and the face bright red.
His tail was spiky and long.
He was fast like a cheetah.
He was as large as five tables
And as tall as the Eiffel Tower and Edinburgh Castle put together.
His breath smelt like cheese and onion crisps with rotten eggs.
He had goo stuck to his teeth,
He moved slowly to get his food.
He ate goo, birds and blood.
His teeth were wobbling,
Ready to eat the goo that was dribbling out of his mouth.

Casey Whyte (9)
Kinghorn Primary School, Kinghorn

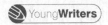

Dragon Poem

Today I saw a dragon
At least 45 feet tall,
And as long as a skyscraper,
Flat on the side.

The dragon's skin
Was as red as boiling lava
And smooth and scaly.

The eyes were very evil-looking,
Staring at me.
They seemed to be the size of
Cannonballs.

His teeth were as white as snow
With a couple of blood stains on them.
They were as sharp as swords,
Ready to bite into my skin.

The breath of the dragon
Stunk of rotten eggs
Or smelly socks or stinky fish,
And every 10 minutes
He would breathe out smoke and fire.

The dragon's movement
Was as fast as a jet,
But silent as a mouse.

Emma Day (9)
Kinghorn Primary School, Kinghorn

The Dragon Poem

Today I saw a dragon,
It nearly scared me to death.
The dragon had massive, bulky, long wings,
It had wet, gooey, dirty, scaly toes.
The dragon was immensely large
With a podgy belly.
His movement was so careful and steady.
The dragon's eyes were like bubbling red lava.
The dragon's nose was squashed and hairy.
You could see he liked a fight
With all the scars and bruises he had.

Vanessa Crowe (9)
Kinghorn Primary School, Kinghorn

The Dragon Poem

I saw a dragon today . . .
It had wings as spiky as the Himalayan Mountains.
The dragon's body was nearly as tall as the world.
His tail was long and swift,
His movement was ever so dashing.
The size of the dragon was immense,
His eyes looked like scorching hot lava.
The texture was bumpy and scaly,
His teeth were gooey, yellow and sharp like razors,
He his green saliva that was dripping out of his mouth,
He had claws as sharp as a dagger.
It looked like he had eaten all the mince pies,
His belly was so big.
His breath was like rotten eggs.

Erin Teasdale (9)
Kinghorn Primary School, Kinghorn

Dragon Poem

Today I saw a dragon,
It had red bloodshot eyes
And gigantic, sharp, fierce teeth.
Its nostrils were spitting out fire,
Like volcanoes about to blow up.
Its body was colossal,
Like an elephant stuffing itself with food.
It was soaring through the air
Like an aeroplane diving at the speed of light.
Its wings were like aeroplane's wings
That could fly forever.

Cameron Doig (9)
Kinghorn Primary School, Kinghorn

A Dragon

Today I saw a dragon,
With bloodshot eyes
And huge, big, yellow teeth,
But it was as fat as the fattest man in the world.
And it was 2000 feet.
It moved as fast as a cheetah,
And its tail wide and sharp as a knife.
The wings were large, scaly and strong,
And that was the dragon I saw today.

Jack Currie (9)
Kinghorn Primary School, Kinghorn

The Dragon

Today I saw a dragon,
Its teeth were blue as goo.
Its body was so scaly
And I found out its name was Bailey.

Its movement was as fast as the speed of lightning.
I don't know how it would fit out of the window
Because it was 45 foot tall.
It must have squeezed its head out of the kitchen window.

The next day I saw Bailey again.
Its wings were as big as 16 windows put together.
It was so big Grandpa couldn't bear it.
Its tail was as red as bubbling lava.

Its head was so big it would fit three 14 full sized-pigs.
My gran came out and screamed for all to help.
Then everyone came outside and saw a flash
And hit a wall, and all everyone heard was *bash!*

David Doig (9)
Kinghorn Primary School, Kinghorn

The Dragon

Today I saw a dragon,
He was fierce and very savage,
He had red skin and was very thin
And broke into my garage.

His head was the size of a double-decker bus,
His foot was as big as a ferry to New York.
His teeth were as sharp as a sword or knife,
I've never seen anything as sharp in my life.

His wings were like leather,
His tail was as solid as a rock.
That's all about the dragon because the army shot him down,
They threw him in the water to make sure he'd drown.

Brian Toal (9)
Kinghorn Primary School, Kinghorn

The Dragon

Today I saw a dragon,
It was gigantic,
It had a rough scaly body,
A spiky brick tail and a hard lumpy head.

Its wings were big and flappy,
Its teeth were as sharp as razors,
And its eyes were as red as fury.

It had long tough legs
with red padding underneath its belly,
It smelt like flames out of a volcano.

When it moved it dashed through the trees
Like it had quick reflexes.
It had lava fire coming out of its mouth,
That was the most amazing thing I'd ever seen.

Cailan Duchain (9)

Kinghorn Primary School, Kinghorn

Battle Of Britain

Thump went the planes, smashing into the ground,
'Ack-Ack', the anti-aircraft guns.
Rubble flying here and there,
Bombs going off, screaming all around.

Crashing of buildings, explosions of planes,
Bombers are going, leaving us just now.
But the shells from over the water
Are coming closer and closer . . .

They stopped after a while,
Leaving destruction where they'd been,
And Britain survived, for another day.

Robin Miles (11)
King's Road Primary School, Rosyth

A Day In The Death Camp

What will happen to us next?
We think all the time,
As we fight to stay alive,
I cry as I write each line.

Over the barbed-wire fences,
People fight for me,
Hitler you've sent us to Hell,
Please let me be free.

Every day I have to work,
Digging the fields,
So tired and hungry,
But I'll get punished if I steal.

My mum sews buttons,
Onto shirts and capes,
But I know someday,
We hope to escape.

Victoria Cretch (11)
King's Road Primary School, Rosyth

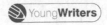

War Is . . .

War is full of innocent people dying
And loads of crying.

War is full of bombs exploding everywhere
And the bombers without a care.

War is full of evacuees
And planes screaming like banshees.

War is full of soldiers, each one with a gun
And the injured children with no fun.

War is full of children's cries
And Hitler's lies.

War is full of dirty tasks
And gas masks.

Megan Ross (11)
King's Road Primary School, Rosyth

Escape from Sobibor

E scape from Sobibor.
S ick people!
C an it be done?
A mazed by all the gunshots,
P ride for their country.
E xcitement as lots of people escaped!

F rightening hearing the gunshots,
R elief as they all get out!
O ff-putting deaths!
M ine fields!

S hooting Jews, lots of people crying!
O ut they all run to escape!
B odies dead, people jumping away!
I mpossible to get out!
B arbed wire ripping people's skin!
O ften people dying from lack of food!
R aging in to the barbed wire!

Jamie Ashmore (11)
King's Road Primary School, Rosyth

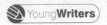

The Dreaded Siren

The dreaded siren goes off,
Horror is what most will feel.
Stukas screaming, booming as the bombs are dropped.

People run to shelter,
People crying as family is dying.
They run as they hear the screech of the gun.

Pilots in the air
Defending our country.
Germany vs Britain in the air!
One plane gone, two, three, Britain is winning.

People still hiding,
Waiting for the all-clear.
Nothing happening.
Then the all-clear goes,
We're safe for another day.

Kirsty Small (11)
King's Road Primary School, Rosyth

Escape from Sobibor

E scape from Sobibor?
S illy idea!
C an't possibly be done.
A ble to die,
P ossible to survive,
E veryone who tries to escape will be killed.

F right is in all of them.
R un away from Sobibor,
O ff into the woods.
M ums and dads crying for their kids.

S ome devastated at the horrors,
O ver three hundred escaped!
B rave people, all of them,
I n the death camps.
B reak the rules and run away,
O ut of this way!
R elief for those who survive.

Jason Biggins (11)
King's Road Primary School, Rosyth

World War II

Smoke travelling in the air,
Explosions from the bombs,
Planes screaming overhead.
There's people everywhere.

Sirens going off at a loud pitch,
Thundering of the guns.
People in the gas chambers,
Some climbing over barbed wire,
Families and friends getting themselves killed.

Swooping of planes just above you,
Horror of the bodies lying there,
Smoke making the sky grey,
Kids crying as they watch their parents being killed.

Nazis killing Jews for no reason,
They're giving orders and shouting out loud.
'Come on, hurry up, get them in the gas chambers.'
People screaming all around, 'Get me out.'

Erin Muir (11)
King's Road Primary School, Rosyth

World War II

Big explosions from the bombs,
People screaming all around,
Smoke making the sky grey,
Sirens going all the time.

Families getting taken apart,
Death camps no one can get out of,
Planes swooping over people's heads,
Thundering of the guns.

Gas chambers with bodies left lying,
Some people hurting themselves climbing over the gates.
Horror of relatives dying in front of people,
Kids crying as they watch the parents being killed.

Jews getting killed for no reason,
Nazis giving orders to the Jews,
People shouting to get out of the gas chambers.

Chloe McIntosh (11)

King's Road Primary School, Rosyth

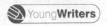

The Battle Of Britain

The siren sounds, they're called to their planes,
The roar of the Spitfire's Mk III Rolls Royce Merlin engine,
Full power down the runway into the sky,
Hurricanes now are following them.
On the radio they are told the enemy's position.

ME109s are escorting their bombers,
The Spitfires have found them with their eagle eyes.
Now the ME109s have spotted them,
The Spitfires fire their 50 calibre Browning machine guns,
German bombers are closing fast.
The Hurricanes take out the bombers,
Hitler's sending no warning!
Ack-Ack guns shoot the planes as well,
Spitfires will never fail!
Bombers plunge into the sea.

The Germans call it the Blitzkrieg,
But it's the finest hour, the battle has begun.
Some planes return to the airfield to be re-armed and re-fuelled,
Some fail and get shot down.

The Hurricanes have shot down the bombers
But the Spitfires have shot down the ME109s.
They still go to check around the channel,
Some find some retreating Germans but they are shot down.

The Spitfires and Hurricanes return to base
And are ready for the next flight . . .

Ben Gourlay (11)
King's Road Primary School, Rosyth

Auschwitz And Sobibor

Auschwitz and Sobibor
Millions died in them
Sadness grabbing at those
Who knew what went on
Yet they laugh and play

Auschwitz and Sobibor
Happiness shone its beams
But they were torn down
Many remember the screams

Auschwitz and Sobibor
Those who escaped
Heard the Germans roar
But they have had their greatest triumph

Auschwitz and Sobibor
Many Jews have died
But their family and friends did not
And so they cried.

Kieran Allcock (11)

King's Road Primary School, Rosyth

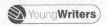

Death Camps

Death camps were horrendous
Soldiers were deplorable to the people
In the camp, so many crestfallen people

Too many unnecessary deaths
Mothers watched as their children
Were brutally murdered

People trying to escape that ghastly place
Attempting to climb over barbed wire

Guns shot across the sand
Whilst hitting everyone in their path
Rationing was diabolical

Terrified to sleep, worrying
That in the morning they would
Be put into the gas chambers.

Chloe Feeney (11)
King's Road Primary School, Rosyth

Camp

The death camps were appalling,
So many lugubrious people
Looking for a way to escape
From these ghastly places.

So many innocent lives were taken
Whilst SS troopers watched,
Delighting in what they saw.

Rations of food were inadequate,
Mothers watching as their
Children were tyrannically
Killed!

Gas chambers were used
On miscellaneous people, gays,
Gypsies, Jews, mentally or physically disabled,
Even children, this was
Diabolical!

Tired and hungry,
Having trouble eating,
But still working for the Germans.

Ashleigh Scott (11)
King's Road Primary School, Rosyth

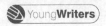

Evacuee

Planes are screaming
I can't get to sleep
Mother is crying
Bombs are falling

'Keep silent,' Mother says
My mask smells horrid
People are being pushed by soldiers
I can't go and play away too far

My suitcase is packed
I get on a train
Mother waves goodbye

I arrive at a big house
A lady is waiting
She is scary
Take me home

A letter comes
Daddy's gone
I cry myself to sleep
No comfort from my mother
Will the war ever end?

Hannah Parker (11)
King's Road Primary School, Rosyth

War

The loud siren goes off,
Anti-aircraft guns firing
With a high groan,
Planes screaming like a banshee.

Bombs tearing up the homes
Of terrified people,
Guns screeching in a high tone,
The voice of battle ringing in their ears.

People dying by the minute,
Allies fighting the Nazis.
Nazi party bombing,
And over-running countries.

The war has been on for years,
Nobody knows when it will be over.
But . . . Britain is not done!

John Adams (11)
King's Road Primary School, Rosyth

Guns And Love

My little girl was born, so fragile yet surviving,
But somehow I feel ashamed
For not letting her know
That her father is no more.

She will be strong and should be carefree,
But she shall not be joyful,
Yet she will not be in sorrow,
She'll just be . . . herself.

It has passed four years,
And she asked, 'Where's my daddy?'
I didn't reply, and she asked.
So then I said, 'He's flying.'

I had to tell her sometime,
So I told my little girl the day after,
I said, 'Your dad was brave and his heart was strong,
But now he's upstairs, way past the clouds,
Sitting with his friends having a jolly time.'

Macaulay McKenna (11)
King's Road Primary School, Rosyth

The Years Of War

Here we stand in the fields
Waiting for the enemy
The signals fired
We are in the war

The Germans attack with mighty tanks
But Britain fights back
The French defend
While America is attacked by Japan

Hitler is horrible, he's killing all the Jews
His concentration camps hold them
Killed in the gas chambers
Families and all

Me and my troops attack the Germans
We have won the war and for evermore.

Heather Michael (11)
King's Road Primary School, Rosyth

A Dream

I lie in my bed at night
Hearing *bang* and *boom,* then *screams,*
I wonder why Hitler can't just let Jews free
To feel the breeze against their cheeks.
I know that this is just a dream,
But I wish it was reality.

Jasmin Fuller (11)

King's Road Primary School, Rosyth

The Children's Big Shock

Before the war the children were free
Running around, happy as can be,
Streets were free from litter,
At night the stars would glitter.
But then the war started,
Bang, bang, boom!

During the war the children were stuck
And their house was a prison, holding them in.
If we leave, it may be deadly,
Hitler's troops will be there, ready
To shoot you down, to the ground,
With no respect for us at all.

The war is over, the children are older,
Many have lost their families,
The Nazis have lost, the allies victorious,
But all my friends who went outside are not here
To see the wrecks of shattered Britain
Where we all live today.

Morgan Maguire (11)
King's Road Primary School, Rosyth

Goodbye Soldier!

I've been in here too long,
I've had enough of this,
I've got to go home now
To my wife and children.

My mother died,
So did my dad,
Help me, help me,
I'm dying.

Is it all over, or is it still on?
I don't know.
I've said my goodbyes
To all my good friends,
But one of my friends
Said, 'You can't leave,
We need you.'

Goodbye soldier.

Erin Letham (11)
King's Road Primary School, Rosyth

The Girl Is A Jew

I am the one who lives in the attic,
It's small, creaky, and we are never allowed out of it.
You've got to be silent, Hitler and the Nazis are coming to hit.

I try to think of the best, I do honestly try,
But my terrified, sad, beautiful mother's emotions run high.
We all painfully start to cry.

There I lie in my bed in a deep sleep,
In my still, quiet room.
Kaboom!
My skeleton shattered,
The screaming air raids have started.

I stagger over to Mama and Papa
And snuggle in.
I just think, *will they ever give in?*

The Nazis charge in, push us out of the house,
Next thing you know you're in a camp surrounded by barbed wire.
You just want to burst out with freedom and get out,
But you can't, you can't.
You now know me as little Miss Anne Frank.

Lana Stevenson (11)
King's Road Primary School, Rosyth

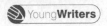

The Tank

Big green and bulky
With its enormous metal tracks
If you try to get it
It will get you back

With a single shot
It can destroy a building
Or destroy a soul
To destroy the Germans
With such a machine
Would be an ultimate goal.

Matthew Bell (11)

King's Road Primary School, Rosyth

I Quit The War For Peace

I quit the war for peace,
Io help families and my friend,
I'll try and hide from this place,
By running round the bend.

I quit the war for peace,
I'm feeling happy for myself,
But also scared at the same time,
Because they might lock me up in a dirty cell.

I quit the war for peace,
Please help me,
I'm hungry and I'm tired,
Just because I quit the army.

Danielle Young (11)
King's Road Primary School, Rosyth

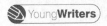

Today I Quit The Army

Today I quit the army,
They don't need me anymore,
I am tired, I am sick,
They don't need me anymore.

I used to hide in holes,
I used to clean shoes,
I used to carry out orders,
I used to clean the loos,
But not anymore.

So today I quit the army,
Indeed I did, indeed I did.

I used to make the food,
I used to eat breakfast on the floor,
I used to hear the air siren going,
But no more.

Today I quit the army, it is the last day,
I will be with the army never again.
I will remember the good times I have had,
World War II is over, they won't need me anymore,
So I can go home again.

Lucy Burns (11)
King's Road Primary School, Rosyth

Bye-Bye Daddy

Bye-bye Daddy,
I'll see you soon,
I'll miss you at home,
And even at school.
And if you die,
Of course I'll cry,
But the main thing is,
You're off to save lives.

Mummy is sad,
So am I,
But we'll get over it,
As long as you don't die.
Everyone is crying,
And half the world is dying,
But the main thing is,
Britain is never lying.

Oh no, oh yes!
I've got the news,
Germany, you're going to lose.
But that's not the point,
You're dead,
My tears shed,
My heart feels also dead.

In my bed,
I can't sleep,
I play with my teddies,
And then I think,
It really is
Bye-bye Daddy.

Megan Stewart (11)
King's Road Primary School, Rosyth

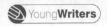

Goodbye

Goodbye my Army,
Goodbye my friends,
I'll miss you all when I'm gone,
So I'm cleaning my rifle one last time,
I'm too old now.
I will remember the good times
And also the bad,
The truck moans and groans,
That's me off for good,
Goodbye, goodbye.

John Grammond (11)
King's Road Primary School, Rosyth

The Story Of War

I'm a pilot
I've flown over France
I've bombed Holland
I'm a pilot

I'm a soldier
I fought many battles
I've been rescued from Dunkirk
I'm a soldier

I'm a sailor
I've saved lives from Dunkirk
I've taken soldiers to Normandy
I'm a sailor

What are you?

Lewis Palmer-Hunt (11)
King's Road Primary School, Rosyth

The Battle Of Britain

The men trained for weeks on end,
Children were sent to the countryside.
Britain was under attack,
So we fought back.
We fought in the skies,
And lots of people died.
The children dressed like Mickey Mouse
To keep them safe from gas.
When the war ended children were free to go home.

Tommy Brown (11)
King's Road Primary School, Rosyth

Poem About Feelings

I'm as happy as a monkey with a load of bananas,
I'm as happy as a pig in a pool of mud,
I'm as lonely as a lizard in an empty desert,
I'm as sad as a mouse without its cheese,
I'm as unhappy as an eagle that's lost its prey,
I'm as happy as a dog that's being brushed,
I'm as sad as a giraffe that can't find its acacia tree,
I'm as lonely as a fish that can't find its shoal.

Ross Anderson (11)
Lumphanan Primary School, Lumphanan

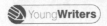

Poem About Feelings

I am as happy as a fish with a nice bowl of clean water
I am as happy as a fox in a chicken coop
I am as lonely as a polar bear in a big grassy meadow
I am as sad as a slug without its slime
I am as unhappy as a shark that's lost its prey
I am as happy as a monkey with a keg that is full of bananas
I am as sad as an elephant that has lost its trunk
I am as lonely as a squirrel without any trees to climb up.

Charlie Whyte (11)
Lumphanan Primary School, Lumphanan

A Poem About Feelings

I'm as happy as a monkey with a bunch of bananas,
I'm as happy as a pig in a pool of mud,
I'm as lonely as a duck in an empty lake,
I'm as sad as an ostrich without its egg,
I'm as unhappy as a squirrel that's lost its nuts,
I'm as happy as a mouse with its cheese,
I'm as sad as a wolf without its pack,
I'm as lonely as a dog in an empty house.

Morgan Alexander (11)
Lumphanan Primary School, Lumphanan

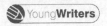

A Poem About Feelings

I'm as happy as a squirrel with a lot of nuts
I'm as happy as a whale in a sea full of plankton
I'm as lonely as a tiger in a cage
I'm as sad as a dog without its family
I'm as unhappy as a monkey that's lost its banana
I'm as happy as a lion with its prey
I'm as sad as a shark in an empty sea
I'm as lonely as a fish with no friends.

Ross Campbell (11)
Lumphanan Primary School, Lumphanan

Dogs

D ogs are cute when chasing their tails,
O ut the door the garden wails.
G ates are opening for them to run,
S omeone is taking them for a walk.

Sophia–Rose James
Meldrum Primary School, Inverurie

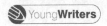

Fox

Silent creeper
Snow hater
Fast eater
Dog hider
Sheep lover
Good fighter
Tail brusher
Forest dweller
Chicken stalker
Water drinker.

Charlie McCann (12)

Meldrum Primary School, Inverurie

Rain

R ain tapping on the roof,
A mazing rainbow colours,
I nteresting puddles reflect the sky,
N o one outside, streets bare.

Rebecca Bruce (11)
Meldrum Primary School, Inverurie

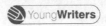

Which Bird?

Fast-runner
Winter-hater
Animal-killer
Night-creeper
Cat-hider
Worm-eater
Spring-lover
Egg-layer
Wood-pecker
Nature-liker.

Jamie White (11)
Meldrum Primary School, Inverurie

Rabbit

Carrot muncher
Water drinker
Happy hopper
Hole digger
Nose twitcher
Food eater
Wire chewer
Ear flopper
Cage sleeper
Poop dropper.

Jordan Johnstone (10)
Meldrum Primary School, Inverurie

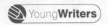

World War II

W orld War II has begun
O verhead you hear the guns being shot
R ed blood lying everywhere
L ove is all around the air
D eath has started

W herever you go you feel unsafe
A ir raid sirens going off everywhere
R ed flames falling from the sky

T housands of people lost their lives
W ill the war ever end?
O ver one and a half million children were evacuated.

Fiona Gower (12)
Muirfield Primary School, Arbroath

Women Start Work

W e are starting work today
O h can't wait to go
M en are at war so we have taken jobs
A woman has never started work
N ow is a big change

S o time to go
T ime to change our life
A terrible thing is what let us start work
R eady to start my new job
T oday is going to be great

W e are starting work today
O h can't wait to go
R eady to start work
K eeping jobs forever is what I will do.

Tammy Price (11)
Muirfield Primary School, Arbroath

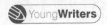

World War II

W hen will the killing end?
O h thy poor British friends
R ussians and Germans and Japanese will pay
L ock and loaded with my sub-machine gun
D oodlebugs come flying into London

W aiting for this war to come to a standstill
A ll the troops' blood is spattered
R aw and red on the grass

T rue sickness and anger inside me
W hen blood is right up to my knees
O h Hitler's dead; killed himself; looks like I'm free, free from it all.

Aiden Cargill (11)
Muirfield Primary School, Arbroath

World War II

W orld War II has begun
O ut the door and into the trenches
R un along no-man's-land
L ife hanging on a piece of thread
D oomsday is here

W inning is impossible
A rmy planes flying overhead
R unning from death

T wo men left
W e all shoot
O ur vision is fading and all I know is death is here.

Joseph Wilson (12)
Muirfield Primary School, Arbroath

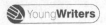

World War II

W ho started World War II?
O h, I know, the Germans,
R ight after they invaded Poland,
L ove and friendship have all gone,
D eath has now begun.

W hen the soldiers sit in their trenches,
A ll freezing cold,
R emember them all.

T here I saw two of our soldiers die,
W hy did they die?
O h why? Oh why?

Nicole Murray (11)
Muirfield Primary School, Arbroath

World War II

W orld War II has begun,
O ver the globe, rifles in hand,
R ed blood and guts all over the trenches,
L ove inside me has gone.
D oes God hate us?

W hy oh why has war started?
A re we unlucky?
R ub the magic lantern and make it end.

T he children draw their chads
W ith the white chalk
O n the brick walls.

Kieran Smith (11)
Muirfield Primary School, Arbroath

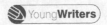

World War II

W ar has started
O ver the hills and beyond
R ed blood everywhere
L ove is gone with my friends
D are myself to cry

W hen I am concentrating I'm thinking
A ll I think of is my family
R eally far away

T wo days of war gone
W ithout my family and friends
O ver I go to war.

Ashley Kerr (11)
Muirfield Primary School, Arbroath

The Mighty Brits And The Blitz

The town o' brown has hit the ground and we all be silent now,
We're hopin' to be safe during' the Blitz, It's drivin' us nutz
Can we really make it again? We only just made it last time,
We were all nearly doomed durin' the Blitz.

Oh the agony's tearin' us apart,
It's breaking' the women and children's hearts.
We're all cow'rin' in the Andy shelter during the Blitz.

Why, why must you make us cry? We just don't want to die,
Me mum's in tears, my dad is dead,
All my brothers fightin' the Germans,
I'm outraged at Hitler now he's makin' us cry and cry.

We will fight on and take the win,
We'll dump Hitler in the bin,
He'll regret fightin' us, for we are the mighty Brits.

Sean Dick (11)
Muirfield Primary School, Arbroath

World War II

W ar has begun, we are the scared ones,
O n trains, others on fighter planes,
R unning into shelters,
L ying in the rubble,
D reaming of happier days.

W aking up in the night,
A ir raid sirens come alive!
R elaxing is hard at this time.

T herefore the war is bad,
W inning is getting so near but yet so far.
O ver and done we have just won!

Carys Boyle (11)
Muirfield Primary School, Arbroath

World War II

W ar has been declared.
O ver the world blood has been shed.
R ight now men are dying for the country.
L ord, what will we do?
D ying for your country will bring you pride.

W itless men are dying for no reason,
A re we dying for no reason?
R oad to war is the biggest but the road out is small.

T orpedoes hit the ships,
W hy? Why?
O ver, the war is over.

Jake Christison (11)
Muirfield Primary School, Arbroath

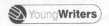

Battle Among The Hell

Green grass turning red,
Among the wounded
Men, they said.
The bombs and torpedoes,
The hell and blood.
Some British fighters among the mud.

The dead men lying
Row on row
In the battlefield that once was home.
In the craters,
Made by the nasty Doodlebugs
From the evil hell-making Nazis.

There is no word to describe
How evil Hitler is,
He got our Churchill in a right fizz!
But now, 70 years on,
We look at the history books
And see how bad it really was.

Greg Robson (11)
Muirfield Primary School, Arbroath

World War II

W ar has started
O bey the rules
R unning to fight
L ights go out
D arkness about.

W hat will happen tonight?
A spot of light, could kill the night,
R un, run, run.

T here is something falling from the sky
W hat is it?
O h, I wonder.

Sydney Thomson (11)
Muirfield Primary School, Arbroath

World War II

W hat awful sights I have seen
O ver the barbed wire fence is the enemy
R ationing for food is such a pain
L onging for the war to end
D eath doesn't frighten me now

W atching the planes flying over our heads
A rmies walking all over Europe
R ed blood all over my hand

T housands of men dying
W hen will the war end?
O h I wish the war was over.

Ross Holder (11)
Muirfield Primary School, Arbroath

World War II

W orld War II has begun.
O ver the trenches I see Nazis,
R ed flames come from the bombs.
L aughing loud, as the Nazis die.
D o we really want war?

W e're all running for our gas masks,
A llies turn into enemies,
R ed Army soldiers come marching in.

T wo enemy planes fly overhead,
W e all hope it's over soon,
O ver five years of fighting finished.

Ethan Bell (11)
Muirfield Primary School, Arbroath

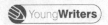

World War II

W ar has started
O ver the world
R unning, shouting, jumping everywhere,
L ooking about to spot a sight,
D ucking down when you hear a *bang!*

W ater, loads of blood everywhere,
A spot of light may light the night,
R acking through the forest.

T rying to win,
W ill I survive?
O r will I die?

Jordyn Rosser (11)
Muirfield Primary School, Arbroath

World War II

W hat is fighting for?
O ver our heads we see the burning planes,
R ed flames flying in the sky,
L aughing out when we see the Nazis die.
D ay by day we see our friends die.

W here are the planes?
A re we not suffering enough?
R un! Or we will die.

T o the people we left behind
W e should kill Hitler when we have time,
O h, what is fighting for?

Ethan Baker (11)
Muirfield Primary School, Arbroath

Bailey And Brandy

B rother lover
A ngel looker
I maginative squeaker
L arge leaper
E nergetic eater
Y oung menace
Bailey

B eer drinker
R abbit leaper
A nimal lover
N ame caller
D ay dreamer
Y our baby
Brandy.

Hannah Pirrie (11)

Pitteuchar West Primary School, Glenrothes

My Dog Alfie

Biscuit-nicker
Rapid-runner
Sneaky-stealer
Loud-woofer
Spectacular-hunter
Smelly-pooper
Sturdy-swimmer
Easy-eater
Chewing-master
Pedigree-pooch
Very-smelly
My best friend!

Jack Szaranek (11)

Pitteuchar West Primary School, Glenrothes

Behind The Door!

Behind that door was a chappy baker,
Who was a great cake maker,
It was Mr Icing.

Sponge, jam and cream
Was his favourite cake dream,
Which was Mr Icing.

'It was yummy, yummy, yummy,
In my tummy, tummy, tummy,'
Said Mr Icing.

Well that's his shop for now,
So say goodbye and take a bow.
'Bye bye,' says Mr Icing.

Caitlin Donald (11)

Pitteuchar West Primary School, Glenrothes

I Might Win

I glide through the water
As graceful as a swan,
It's just touched me
That I might win.

I've got two more lengths,
I've got to go, go, go.
It's just rushed me
That I might win.

I'm way ahead and I hear
The audience scream, 'You're nearly there Callum!'
It's just pushed me
That I might win.

I'm gonna do it for my mum,
My gran and all my family.
It's just excited me
That I might win.

I'm nearly there, I'm sliding slowly,
Down the pool, I eye my enemy.
It's starting to scare me
That I might win.

I touch the wall,
I've got a good time.
I'm really happy
That I *have* won!

Callum Smith (11)
Pitteuchar West Primary School, Glenrothes

Behind The Door

Behind the door no one knows,
Could be a spider or a giant troll.
No sunlight, no fun, what could it be
Behind this door where it has no sun?

Is it a spider or is it a troll?
Like I said, no one knows.
Heavens above and Hell no fury,
Behind this door is something imaginary.

Something nice, something kind,
Could be a pony behind.
Could be space at the door
With burning stars shimmering so brightly in the sky.

Open the door, don't be afraid,
It could be your gran having milk and cookies - hooray!
I open the door,
Where it was my hamster having fun in the sun.

Natalie Connelly (11)
Pitteuchar West Primary School, Glenrothes

Land And Sea

Sea
Peaceful, fun
Blue, noisy, beautiful
Sea stuff, land stuff
Playing, diving, floating
Sunbathing, reading
Land.

Katie Rafferty (8)
St Joseph's RC School, Aberdeen

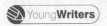

Sea And Land

Sea
Blue, watery
Soft, crashing, peaceful
The wet sea, the dry land
Swaying, noisy, multicultural
Sunny, rainy
Land.

Leston D'costa (8)

St Joseph's RC School, Aberdeen

Lions

Lions run very fast.
Lions are cool.
Lions have sharp teeth.
Lions have sharp claws.
Lions are very loud.
Lions are very fierce.
Lions have big feet.
Lions are wild.

Cameron Roe–Henderson (8)
St Joseph's RC School, Aberdeen

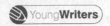

Sporty And Lazy

Sporty
Strong, active
Running, jumping, swimming
The sporty stuff, the lazy stuff
Lying, eating, TV
Weak, slow
Lazy.

Sabine Culligan
St Joseph's RC School, Aberdeen

Japan— Haiku

Amazing and great,
Fabulous and beautiful,
Ancient and modern.

Callum Holland (9)
St Joseph's RC School, Aberdeen

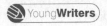

The Dino

Claw-crasher
Loud-roarer
Food-stealer
Terrible-lizard
Human-eater
A big monster.

Gailash Ruthirakumar (8)
St Joseph's RC School, Aberdeen

The Sea

T he sea is very peaceful.
H ave fun in the sea.
E xplore the sea.

S eahorses and dolphins.
E lectric eels.
A mazing shells.

Alia Bedawi (8)

St Joseph's RC School, Aberdeen

Squirrel

Nut-eater
Trick-performer
Clever-thinker
Tree-climber
Great-hider
Fur-wearer
Quick-runner
High-jumper
Cheeky-player
A rare find.

Charlotte Rutherford (8)
St Joseph's RC School, Aberdeen

A Fantastic Acrostic

S ea creatures are strange, weird and prickly.
E lectric eels are a bit like slugs.
A n octopus has eight legs.

C rabs have claws to grab their prey.
R ocks in the sea are called corals.
E very sea creature eats different fish.
A ny jellyfish moves very slowly.
T entacles can be stingy.
U nder the sea live lots of creatures.
R unning sea creatures like lobsters run a bit slow.
E very crab and lobster has a small mouth.
S eaweed grows very fast but gets eaten.

Lachlan Craw (8)

St Joseph's RC School, Aberdeen

When They Came

A normal day?
Or so it seemed,
Playing in the street happily, with friends,
Unaware,
So innocent!

When they came,
Bang! Bang!
Bombs boom! Boom!
Falling, falling
All night like the sun wasn't there.
Frightening!
Scary!
Terror!
Run - the Nazis are coming!
Run - the Nazis are coming!

When they came
Into the Anderson shelter
Praying for dear God,
The smell was like burning rubber.
I heard screams and bombs,
I saw total darkness.
I felt terrified.
Sadness!
Sadness!
When they came.

When I heard the all clear siren,
Relief.
No party, no cheers,
Complete silence.
Horror!
Darkness!
Obliteration!

Aaron Skene (10)
Scotstown School, Bridge of Don

That Day

One normal day
Playing
Happy
Until
That day
Buzz buzz buzz!
A carpet of black filled the sky
We ran to the Anderson shelter
Bang bang!
That day

Horror
Terrified
Then I heard it
I heard the all clear siren
I got out of the Anderson shelter
Horrifying
Terrifying
That day.

Laura Laird (10)

Scotstown School, Bridge of Don

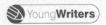

The Day They Came

In my room
What's that noise?
It sounds like buzzing like bees
Planes fill the sky like clouds
As black as coal
I knew it had started
The day they came.

Bang!
Horns and sirens were on
And mum rushed downstairs
Into the Anderson shelter
The day they came.

It was dark and creepy and old
Bang! Boom!
Terrified!
Shocked!
Exhausted!

In the morning
Everything was quiet
All clear siren
Relief
Horror!
Sadness!
But I knew they would be back soon.

Adam Matthew (11)
Scotstown School, Bridge of Don

Blitz Poem

In the field
Playing happily
What was that noise?
It sounded like wasps were buzzing
I saw planes going in the sky
They were black and grey
It was the Nazis' planes
I heard the siren
The siren
Terrified!
To the Anderson shelter
I had gone inside it
I heard the planes dropping bombs
Fear!
The bomb exploded
Bang!
The bomb sounded like
A banging noise
The planes had gone away
Relief!

Tiger Qian (10)
Scotstown School, Bridge of Don

Evacuation

Evacuation, evacuation, where are we going?
Are we going to the countryside?
Is there someone caring?
The bloodshed of war was like a lion tearing the head off its prey,
When will we go home? Please let it be soon.
Until this war is over everyone is in danger,
This war will be gruesome
War was just Hell.

Logan McKinlay (10)
Scotstown School, Bridge of Don

Doomsday!

A normal day
Or so it seemed
Playing outside
People walking their dogs
Silent
Doomsday!

A sudden siren came out of nowhere
Like a wailing banshee
That was when we saw them
The Nazis were coming
A 'V' shape of evil crows above
Fear!
Doomsday!

It was a vision from Hell
Boom!
Crash!
Went the bombs
One by one
Went the houses
Destruction!
Death!
Doomsday!

The all clear siren came on
Relief!
There were no celebrations
Nothing
Only silence
And we knew one thing
They would be back
Doomsday!

Jodie Maxwell (10)
Scotstown School, Bridge of Don

The Bad Blitz For The Brits

A normal day
Or so it seemed
Me and my family were so sweet
And then it came
Happiness interrupted
The bad Blitz for the Brits.

A siren wailed like the loudest thing I'd ever heard
A humming noise like a swarm of wasps
Coming closer!
Coming closer!
Coming closer!
I looked out my window and the sky was black
A black carpet of spiders filled the air
And then it came
The bad Blitz for the Brits.

Into the Anderson shelter!
Into the Anderson shelter!
Bang! Bang! Bang!
Scream!
Scream!
Terror!
Death!
Destruction!
And then it came
The bad Blitz for the Brits.

Amy Brodie (10)
Scotstown School, Bridge of Don

Pick Me

As I stand on the platform
I feel the breeze gently blowing against my face
As I look around, doctors, lawyers and more
Take their pick out of the children.

I think to myself
What should I do? Should I run or stay?
I miss my family so much
It feels as if my heart has been pulled out
I saw my brother get picked
Will anyone pick me?

I taste the taste of fear
And shivers tingle down my spine
Who will pick me?
A doctor, lawyer, farmer, shopkeeper, milkman?
Who? Who will? Who will pick me?

Kirsty Pratt (10)
Scotstown School, Bridge of Don

That Day

My friends and I
Playing unaware
A normal day
Or so I thought
Buzz! Buzz!
They were here
My friend and I
Ran
The siren, the siren
In the Anderson shelter
Bang! Bang! Scream!
My heart was thumping like a frog
Terror!
Torture!
Death!
That day
I heard bombs screaming
I smelt rubber
I saw nothing but darkness
I felt petrified
Siren
They were gone
Siren wailed like a banshee
Relief
No cheers
No parties
We knew they'd be back
No happiness
Only sorrow
That day.

Chloe Reid (10)

Scotstown School, Bridge of Don

A Cry For Life

Running in the garden
Innocent as can be
Take a drink
The bottle shakes
Puzzled wonder at first
The terror
The Germans!
The Germans!
'Be quiet my dear!' my mother yells
'Please come here,' I cry
Oh my!
The floor shakes
Then I see it
A vision from Hell
Like beetles flying in the sky
The Germans have bombs! The Germans have bombs!
'Get in the Anderson shelter,' my mother screamed
I scramble in terror
I can smell fuel
Boom! The first bomb goes off
Terror!
Chills!
Destruction!
On and off for many hours
Like locusts never going away
Then it stops
Silence
No cheers
No parades
All silent
Fear!
Destruction!

Connull Drummond (10)
Scotstown School, Bridge of Don

That Dreaded Night

It was that shocking night
On the way to the butcher's
That dreadful, buzzing sound
Finally I saw them
Suddenly the siren wailed in fear
Shock!
Running round until
I knew it was real
Death!
Destruction!
That dreaded night.

Bombs coming down like rain
Weeeee! Phrrrph!
I heard the boom
I saw only darkness
I felt a whisper in my ear
It would be alright
Would it?
On that dreaded night.

Finally I heard it
The all clear siren
Then silence
Nothing but silence
The evil black crows had gone
But would they be back?
That dreaded night.

Casey Blyth (10)
Scotstown School, Bridge of Don

Evacuee Evacuation

E very day I wake up I get this funny feeling,
V elns tIngling in my blood and then I get believing
A nd I go outside to the sight of my eyes, a fighter jet above,
C ue the sight I'd like to love.
U sing the sight that is really blinding
E vacuation not for me, I better get hiding.
E very second of the day eating corned beef,

E at, eat, eat, they shout 'Yum,' I believe.
V ery strong smell of smoke running over the hill
A n unexploded grenade, *boom* it goes, *boom* when I touch it.
C utting the wire for the light
U sing the time to hide away
A bsolute pitch-black.
T ouching and feeling the darkness
I feel strange, I feel brave.
O n the train my friends all go,
N ot for me evacuation (too sad).

Emily Bain (9)
Scotstown School, Bridge of Don

The Day They Came

A normal day
Or so it seemed
Bang!
The Nazis
Bang!
I was scared
Swish then a bang
What should I do?
The Nazis were coming
The Nazis were coming
To the Anderson shelter
Praying for our lives
The Nazis were coming
The Nazis were coming
Terror!
Death!
Then it was all over
No parties
No cheers
Just sorrow.

Stephen McStay (10)
Scotstown School, Bridge of Don

The Day Of Death

Oh that day
That horrifying day
The day of
Terror from Hell

In the park
Playing with friends
A day of innocence and joy
Or was it?
Then a sound
A humming sound
Buzz! Buzz! Buzz!
Like terrifying bees
The Germans are here
The Germans are here
The Germans are here to kill
A blanket of terror arrived
Death!
Shock!
Run!
To the underground station
Boom! Boom!
Like a display of fireworks
Then the siren
The calming siren
The all clear siren
No voices
Nothing
Just silence
We knew they would come again

On that day
That horrifying day
The day of
Terror from Hell.

Aishwarya Harish (10)
Scotstown School, Bridge of Don

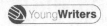

Egypt

Egypt is hot
Egypt is sunny
Pyramids are high
And that's so funny

Pharaohs wear cloaks
Not like other folks
They wear kilts
Sometimes a flower wilts

Then we come to Rameses
He was really great
He was very light for his weight

He had a gold ring around his neck
It was more delicate than a little bird's peck.

Jake Zebedee (8)

Scotstown School, Bridge of Don

The Night And Me

Everyone is asleep, you couldn't hear a peep
But the night and me are not even asleep
We are still playing and chatting
Soon we get sleepy
My mum calls me in
She says, 'Where have you been?'
I say, 'I have been playing with the night.'

Molly Rennie (8)
Scotstown School, Bridge of Don

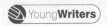

The Snowy Day

The sun is hot.
The snow is cold.
It is cold here
And all the animals are
Finding a place to hide.
It is hot in another
Country.

Blaine McKinlay (8)

Scotstown School, Bridge of Don

Jack

Jack, thin, unhappy young boy.
Snowdrop eyes which have sunk into his bleak, black face.
His crooked young back is bent like a man of one hundred.
His hands are black bones without skin.
He struggles on his knees,
Moving ever so slightly.
Then suddenly
He stops.
The weeping of young children disturbs him.
He keeps moving.
Not because he wants to,
Because he has to.

Ellie Laurie (8)
Scotstown School, Bridge of Don

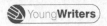

Upside Down

Upside down, upside down
It's so great to be upside down.
I go upside down,
I do it all the time.
I don't care if it's time
To go to bed.
I sleep upside down
And even listen to my teacher
Upside down.
I cycle home upside down
And walk the
Dog upside down.
What I am trying to say is,
I've spent my life upside down.

Lewis Brooks (8)

Scotstown School, Bridge of Don

Clever

(Inspired by 'Predictable' by Bruce Lansky)

Poor as an orphan,
Strong as a monster truck,
Cute as a dog,
Smart as a computer.

Thin as a pencil lead,
White as Dracula,
Fit as a sportsman,
Dumb as Homer Simpson.

Long as a limo,
Short as a hippo,
Hard as a table,
Munchy as a crunchy.

Bald as a turkey,
Neat as a suit,
Proud as a winner,
Ugly as a frog.

Fast as a cheetah,
Slow as a turtle,
Quiet as a mouse,
Bright as the sun.

Use fresh similes when
You talk and write,
So your friends think you're
Clever and bright.

Cameron Ewen (9)
Scotstown School, Bridge of Don

Clever

(Inspired by 'Predictable' by Bruce Lansky)

Poor as a wallet with no money,
Strong as the world's strongest man,
Cute as a kitten,
Smart as a calculator.

Thin as a page of a book,
White as a sheet on the washing line,
Fit as a gymnast,
Dumb as a goldfish.

Bald as a grandad,
Neat as someone signing a letter,
Proud as a gymnast winning gold,
Ugly as a toad.

Soft as a cushion,
Hard as rock,
Fast as a jet,
Slow as a turtle.

Use fresh similes when
You speak and write,
So your friends think you are
Quite clever and bright.

Lily McLeod (10)
Scotstown School, Bridge of Don

Clever

(Inspired by 'Predictable' by Bruce Lansky)

Poor as Woolworths,
Strong as a plane,
Cute as a kitten,
Smart as a calculator.

Thin as a crayon,
White as a cloud,
Fit as a sportsman,
Dumb as a goldfish.

Bald as a frog,
Neat as a suit,
Proud as a lion,
Ugly as a scorpion.

Fast as a leopard,
Slow as a worm,
Bright as the sun,
Quiet as a rat.

Use fresh similes when
You speak and write,
So you friends will think you are
Quite clever and bright.

Aditya Suvarna (9)
Scotstown School, Bridge of Don

Clever

(Inspired by 'Predictable' by Bruce Lansky)

Poor as an orphan,
Strong as a plane,
Cute as a puppy,
Smart as a cheetah.

Thin as a toothpick,
White as a polar bear,
Fit as a lion,
Dumb as Patrick Star.

Bald as Homer Simpson,
Neat as a limo,
Proud as parents on their birthdays,
Ugly as an alien.

Wet as a flooded house,
Quiet as a TV on mute,
Pretty as a rose,
Fun as Florida's theme parks.

Use fresh similes
When you speak or write,
So your friends will think you are
Quite clever and bright.

Jade Durno (9)
Scotstown School, Bridge of Don

Clever

(Inspired by 'Predictable' by Bruce Lansky)

Poor as a beggar,
Strong as the army,

Smart as a textbook.

Thin as a twig,
White as a snowball,

Dumb as Homer Simpson.

Bald as a hairless man,
Neat as a limo,

Ugly as a troll.

Quiet as a mouse,
Loud as a lion,

Cheeky as a monkey.

Use fresh similes when
You speak and write,
So your friends will think you are
Quite clever and bright.

Rachel Milne (9)
Scotstown School, Bridge of Don

Clever

(Inspired by 'Predictable' by Bruce Lansky)

Poor as Woolworths,
Strong as dynamite,
Cute as a kitten,
Smart as an ape.

Thin as a pencil,
White as a person with frostbite,
Fit as a penguin,
Dumb as Homer Simpson.

Bald as a cow,
Neat as a suit,
Proud as Alexandra Burke,
Ugly as a pig.

Fat as a hippo,
Cheeky as Bart Simpson,
Rubbish as My Little Pony,
Brainy as Lisa Simpson.

Tall as a giraffe,
Small as a mouse,
Fast as a cheetah,
Slow as a turtle.

Ace as a monkey,
Green as grass,
Friendly as a dog,
Stunning as a castle.

Giggly as a hyena,
Beautiful as a butterfly,
Pink as skin,
Red as lava.

Use fresh similes when
You speak and write,
So your friends will think you are
Clever and bright.

Ross Chouman (10)
Scotstown School, Bridge of Don

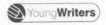

Clever

(Inspired by 'Predictable' by Bruce Lansky)

Poor as Woolworths,
Strong as a boxer,
Cute as a baby,
Smart as a computer.

Thin as a pencil,
White as a snowball,
Fit as a sportsman,
Dumb as Homer Simpson.

Bald as an egg,
Neat as a hotel room,
Proud as a football team winning a cup,
Ugly as a troll.

Bright as a bulb,
Fast as an Olympic 100m champion,
Quite as a mute,
Slow as a snail.

Use fresh similes when
You speak and write,
So your friends will think you are
Quite clever and bright.

Ewan Davidson (9)
Scotstown School, Bridge of Don

Clever

(Inspired by 'Predictable' by Bruce Lansky)

Poor as a man on a street,
Strong as a strong man,
Cute as a rabbit,
Smart as an answer book.

Thin as a pencil,
White as a snowflake,
Fit as a runner,
Dumb as a dummy.

Bold as a fish,
Neat as my friends,
Proud as a singer,
Ugly as a wart monster.

Quiet as a spy,
Dark as the night sky,
Loud as a bullhorn,
Light as the sun.

Use fresh similes when
You speak and write,
So your friends will think you are
Quite clever and bright.

Jade Ramsay (9)
Scotstown School, Bridge of Don

Clever

(Inspired by 'Predictable' by Bruce Lansky)

Poor as an orphan,
Strong as a crane,
Cute as a cat,
Smart as a computer.

Thin as a piece of paper,
White as a snowflake,
Dumb as a headless chicken.

Bald as a potato,
Neat as dry-cleaned clothes,
Proud as a new father,
Ugly as a monster.

Use fresh similes when
You speak and write,
So your friends will think you are
Quite clever and bright.

Jack Gillies (9)
Scotstown School, Bridge of Don

Clever

(Inspired by 'Predictable' by Bruce Lansky)

Poor as a person with no house,
Strong as a bear,
As smart as a computer,
Cute as a dolphin in the sea somewhere.

Thin as a blade of grass,
White as a polar bear in the snow,
Fit as a lion,
Silly as a rat doing a tap-dancing show.

Bald as an egg,
Neat as a tidy bedroom,
Proud as a mother and father of their daughter in a show,
Ugly as Cinderella's stepsisters with broken legs.

Fast as a runner at the Olympics,
Quiet as a mouse,
Slow as a snail,
Messy as my house.

Use fresh similes
When you speak and write,
So your friends will think you are
Quite clever and bright.

Rebecca Wilson (9)
Scotstown School, Bridge of Don

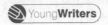

Clever

(Inspired by 'Predictable' by Bruce Lansky)

Poor as a beggar,
Strong as an earthquake,
Cute as a cub,
Smart as a calculator.

Thin as a strand of hair,
White as a whiteboard,
Fit as a football player,
Dumb as a chimp.

Bald as an egg,
Neat as a trophy,
Proud as a team winning a cup,
Ugly as a dead bird.

Messy as a plate of jelly,
High as a mountain,
Low as a chair,
Long as a wall.

Use fresh similes when
You speak and write,
So your friends will think you are,
Quite clever and bright.

Saqib Rasul (9)
Scotstown School, Bridge of Don

Clever

(Inspired by 'Predictable' by Bruce Lansky)

Poor as people that don't have a bank account,
Strong as a wrestler,
Cute as a newborn baby,
As smart as a 100 brains in one person's head.

Thin as a lead,
As white as a whiteboard,
Fit as a football player,
Dumb as a person that doesn't know 1+1.

Bold as an elephant,
Neat as a very tidy desk tidy,
Proud as an X Factor winner,
Ugly as my baby sister.

As messy as jelly,
As sharp as a knife,
As high as Big Ben,
As low as my cousin's house.

Use fresh similes when
You speak and write,
So your friends will think you are
Quite clever and bright.

Yusuf Sarwar (9)
Scotstown School, Bridge of Don

Clever

(Inspired by 'Predictable' by Bruce Lansky)

Poor as a church mouse,
Strong as a bull,
Cute as a kitten,
Smart as a fox.

Thin as a toothpick,
White as a sheet of paper,
Fit as a sportsman,
Dumb as a plank of wood.

Bald as a bald man,
Neat as a suit,
Proud as a singer,
Ugly as my sister.

Use fresh similes
When you speak or write,
So your friends will think you are,
Quite clever and bright.

Craig Esson (9)
Scotstown School, Bridge of Don

Horse

Hay eater
Tail swisher
Happy bucker
Apple stealer
Hoof beater
Fast runner
Good jumper
Soft fur
Fluffy mane
Nice friend.

Charlotte Clarke (8)

Strachan Primary School, Banchory

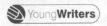

The Storm

Tumbling, thumbling, crashing down, never knowing
What to do,
Don't stop,
Don't go,
Don't let it snow!

Zoe Barton (8)

Strachan Primary School, Banchory

The Storm

Splash, slosh, splashing,
Wet and rainy,
Howling, rumbling, screeching,
It is like the Devil is coming.

Jenny Gillies (9)
Strachan Primary School, Banchory

The Storm

The wind whistles
The thunder roars
The lightning flashes
The lightning crashes
The wet drops of rain
On my head
Will soak me through
Until I am dead.

Morven MacFarlane (9)
Strachan Primary School, Banchory

Wolf

Storm grey
Quiet as air
Fast as a spirit
The sign of strength
Stealth!

Ewen Kerridge (11)
Strachan Primary School, Banchory

Storm

Shocking thunder, splattering rain,
All the way down the lane.
Crashing thunder,
Bright flashing lightning,
It is all very frightening.
Hurricane, tornado, snow,
We all want it to go.
It is all fading away now,
It is a sunny day.
Hip hip hooray.

Thomas Daines (8)

Strachan Primary School, Banchory

The Storm

Crashing and trashing the earth
Tearing and gnawing the bark
The storm appears

Whipping and thawing the earth
Mad winds from north, east, south and west
The storm starts to rage

Trees fly from overhead
While forest creatures dive for cover
The storm comes nearer

Typhoons rage
While branches are torn off remaining trees
The storm is here.

Findlay Randalls (9)
Strachan Primary School, Banchory

Rumbling Grumbling Storm

Hear the rumbling
Hear the grumbling
Trees a-tumbling
Wind a-howling
A storm is going on

Rain a-beating
Pouring breathing
Crumbling heaving
Time is leaving
A storm is going on

There's a bash
There's a crash
See the flash
Feel the bash
A storm is going on.

Anna Barton (10)
Strachan Primary School, Banchory

Ice Skater

Cool
Sparkling clear
Shimmering, sprinkling ice
The ice glows when she skates
Amazing jumping girl
Twirly, stretchy
Skater.

Nicole Smith (10)
Strachan Primary School, Banchory

The Storm

Howling, thrashing, roaring
The storm comes nearer.

Thundering, grumbling, beating
The storm comes nearer.

Crashing, splashing, growling
The storm comes nearer.

Little trees falling, big ones groaning
The storm is here.

Raging, pouring, tipping
The storm is angry.

Still tumbling, still thrashing
But the storm's going away.

Everything's dripping, everything soaking
But the storm's gone.

Evan MacFarlane (11)
Strachan Primary School, Banchory

Penguins

The majestic penguin roams the land of Antarctica,
Waddling to their home in-between the tall ice walls
Before coming back to fish in the sea.
All the penguins in the water glide without a care,
Fishes swim away in all directions but are caught,
They swim away into the icy horizon
Where they go to fish some more.

Fernando Greatbatch (11)
Strathdon School, Strathdon

Panda

Panda
Furry, cuddly
Bamboo eating friend
You will always know
He'll be there
Forever eating
Eating.

Alexander Gray (11)
Strathdon School, Strathdon

Robots

Clang-bang
Clever-machine
Flies-talks
Fixing-devices
Oiled-joints
Shiny-metal
Ingenious-robots.

Rowan Currie (10)
Strathdon School, Strathdon

Budgies

Cheep cheeper
Feather leaver
Sleep sleeper
Beak pecker
TV watcher
Wing flapper
Fly flier
Food eater
Water drinker.

Sean Taylor (10)
Strathdon School, Strathdon

Random

Bees like pie,
So do I.
Foxes are sly,
I don't know why.
I hope pigs fly,
But they'd take up the sky.
Pigs fly high,
Bees eat pie,
And I still don't know why.
Foxes are sly.

Rory Dobson (10)
Strathdon School, Strathdon

Tyrannosaurus

T eeth like carving knives,
Y ou'll be swallowed whole.
R ooooaaaar!
A ll creatures are food,
N o beast rivals it,
N o beast survives its attack.
O h no! It's coming!
S uch a mighty predator,
A meteorite hits the Earth.
U tter madness breaks out,
R uler of the dinosaurs is alone,
U nderstand it's on its own.
S uddenly it's extinct.

Scott Foreman (9)
Strathdon School, Strathdon

Dragons

D eadly beasts!
R oar, roar, roar!
A wful bad breath!
G reedy things they are!
O range fire they will blow!
N aughty ones for playing tricks!
S team is coming from their nostrils!

Ewan Eddie (10)

Strathdon School, Strathdon

Harley Davidson

Two-wheeler
Fun-traveller
Smooth-rider
Leather-seater
Engine-shaker
Wind-cutter
Thunder-sounder
Easy-turner
A good vehicle!

Amber Walsh (11)
Strathdon School, Strathdon

Rabbit

Sweet-fluffy
Jumping-cuddler
Carrot-eater
Running-danger
Happy-player
Sleeping-well.

Neive Tough (10)
Strathdon School, Strathdon

Dragon

There was a dragon
Who could not blow fire.
So he fell in a wagon
And hit barbed wire.

Daragh Tough (9)
Strathdon School, Strathdon

Young Writers Information

We hope you have enjoyed reading this book - and that you will continue to enjoy it in the coming years.

If you like reading and writing poetry drop us a line, or give us a call, and we'll send you a free information pack.

Alternatively if you would like to order further copies of this book or any of our other titles, then please give us a call or log onto our website at www.youngwriters.co.uk

Young Writers Information
Remus House
Coltsfoot Drive
Peterborough
PE2 9JX
(01733) 890066